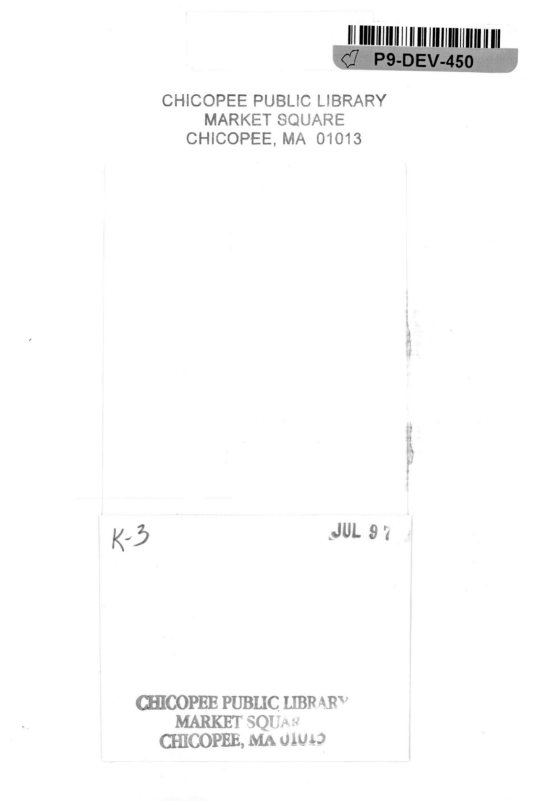

# AMERICAN INDIAN FOODS

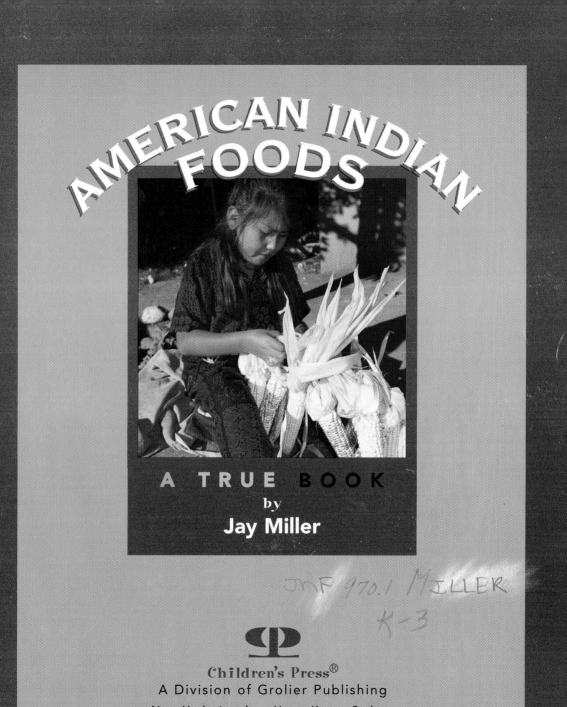

## A TRUE BOOK

by
**Jay Miller**

**Children's Press®**
A Division of Grolier Publishing
New York  London  Hong Kong  Sydney
Danbury, Connecticut

For help in reading and writing these books, Jay Miller thanks Sara, Harry, and Anne.

*Reading Consultant*
**Linda Cornwell**
*Learning Resource Consultant*
*Indiana Department of*
*Education*

Library of Congress Cataloging-in-Publication Data

Miller, Jay, 1947-
    American Indian foods / by Jay Miller.
        p.    cm. — (A true book)
    Includes bibliographical references and index.
    Summary: Briefly describes some of the foods that were important to various North American Indian cultures and rituals surrounding their harvesting, hunting, food preparation, and meals.
    ISBN 0-561-20135-2 (lib.bdg.)        ISBN 0-516-26091-X (pbk.)
    1. Indians of North America—Food—Juvenile literature.  [1. Indians of North America—Food. 2. Indians of North America—Social life and customs] I. Title. II. Series.
E98.F7M55  1996
641.59'297—dc20                                                    96-13476
                                                                          CIP
                                                                          AC

# Contents

Corn growing in a dry area

# Ways of Living

American Indians relied on their many different home-lands for the foods they needed. Each tribe had its own ways to get, store, and cook food.

Throughout North America, foods were either taken from nature or planted and harvested in fields. In different areas, different foods were staples—they were the basic food for everyone. Corn, beans, and squash were staples in the South and East, for example, while salmon was a staple in the Northwest.

In the West and North, tribes lived by harvesting seeds, nuts, berries, and roots, and by hunting animals. In the East and South, farmers worked in fields to grow corn,

Squash and sunflowers are native to North America.

beans, squash, sunflowers, and other crops. Everywhere, people worked together to harvest and store food.

Arctic Ocean

Inuit

Inuit

Inuit

# Northwest Coast

Pacific Ocean

Cheyenne
## Plains

## Great Lakes
Iroquois

Numa

Navajo

Shawnee

Pueblo
## Southwest

Atlantic Ocean

NORTH AMERICAN TRIBES

Gulf of Mexico

Caribbean Sea

# Knowing How

Over thousands of years, people learned the best ways to live in their homelands. They learned where the best wild foods grew and when they were ripe. They learned how to grow many crops in fields.

Hunters knew the ways of animals. Often they could guide an animal to a path or stream bank before they killed it, where it would be easier to cut up and bring home. Once the meat was taken, they knew how to dry and preserve it.

People also knew to be grateful. When foods became available, each was welcomed with prayers and rituals. Every staple food in the Americas was treated to one of the Return Foods Rituals of Thanksgiving.

Because there were no grocery stores or money, every

People in special costumes dance to thank the corn (above). Baskets are still made by hand today (right).

family also made many of the things it needed to live. Men made tools from stone, wood, leather, shell, and horn. Women made clothes, baskets, pots, pans, and string.

# Gathering Food

In some places, American Indian people lived on a staple food that they gathered from nature. Of course, they also gathered other foods and hunted animals.

In California, the staple was acorns. Families owned oak groves and shared them with

Acorns have hard shells that must be removed before they can be ground into flour.

relatives and friends. Men climbed the trees to shake loose the acorns, and women collected them. But raw acorns have a poison inside, so the women ground them up and ran hot water through the flour to wash it away. They stored the powder and some whole acorns for the winter.

At meal times, the mother made a soup, mush, or bread of this acorn flour. Sometimes she flavored it with meat, fish, or berries.

In what is now Nevada and Utah, the staple of the Numa people was pinyon pine nuts, but many different kinds of food had to be used. Foods

Pine nuts in woven baskets

there were scattered and water was scarce. People also collected, cooked, and powdered many kinds of insects for food. Later in the year, seeds were gathered, roasted, and stored.

Throughout the Great Lakes, fish and wild rice were the staples. Wild rice is a water plant with rice-like seeds, not really a kind of rice. It grows in clear, slow-moving water.

Families owned patches of these plants. At harvest time

16

in the fall, they marked their patches by twisting and decorating bunches of the plants. A man poled a canoe through the water while a woman bent the bunches down and knocked the rice seeds off and into the canoe with sticks.

The seeds were dried and roasted, then tossed gently into the air, so that the wind blew away the husks. This is called winnowing. The seeds were stored for the winter and used in soups and stews.

# Catching Salmon

In the Pacific Northwest, where people lived very well off the foods of the forest, sea, and shore, salmon was the staple. Every year, salmon swam up the rivers to lay eggs. Using nets, spears, and fences across rivers called weirs, people caught many

Men catch salmon from the river with nets on long poles (top). Fish are also caught when they swim into these traps (left).

fish during these runs. Everyone labored all day long for weeks to catch, slice, dry, and store these delicious fish.

Salmon must be dried and smoked before it can be stored.

Along the Pacific, each salmon returned only once; they died after laying their eggs. Atlantic salmon, caught by East Coast natives, came back for several years in a row before they died. Shad, char, and other fish also arrived in large numbers and were taken and dried.

# Hunting Seal

In the far north, the Inuit lived off fish, caribou, and other foods. The staple of the Inuit of the Canadian Arctic was the seal.

Seals must come up to the surface of the water to breathe. In the winter, the ocean is frozen over, and so seals keep breathing holes—

Snowmobiles pull caribou on these sleds. Once, sled dogs performed this work.

called blow holes—open through the ice.

To catch a seal, a hunter looked for a blow hole. There, the hunter waited patiently, dressed to be warm even while standing still in the freezing cold.

Sometimes after hours of waiting, a seal would surface. The hunter at once plunged a harpoon into the seal and held on to a cord tied to the point of the harpoon. The point dug in, and the seal could not pull free.

When the seal died, the hunter enlarged the ice hole and pulled it out. In thanks, the hunter gave the seal a

Hunters get ready to move a seal they have killed.

drink of fresh water, a special favor because these animals live in salt water. The meat was always shared with everyone who lived nearby, because food was hard to find in the Arctic.

# Hunting Buffalo

The Plains, in the middle of North America, once were filled with grasslands. The bison, usually called buffalo, ate this grass. It was the largest land animal of the continent—bulls (male bison) could weigh over a ton.

Huge herds filled the region and fed many tribes. Every

A herd of buffalo graze in South Dakota (above). Grass grew back greener after fires like this on the Plains (right).

year, people set fires to keep the grasses fresh and green for the buffalo. Fresh meat to eat right away was taken with spears or bows and arrows. Most meals, however, featured dried meat, taken during yearly hunts by the camp or town.

Some tribes used places called buffalo jumps to get their meat for the year. Men and women made noise and waved robes to scare a herd

The Cheyenne needed the buffalo for more than food. This knife is made from a buffalo rib.

over a high cliff, the buffalo jump. At the bottom, women butchered the buffalo and cut them up to make dried meat.

Five hundred years ago, the Spanish came to America. They brought the horse.

Indian nations of the Plains
learned to admire and use
the horse. On horseback,
they could shoot only those
buffalos they wanted to kill.

Buffalo were still
hunted for food one
hundred years ago.

# Planting and Tending Crops

Over thousands of years, the people of North America learned how to farm. Corn, beans, and squash became staples in the South and East. Iroquois of modern New York called these plants the "three sisters" because they planted them together. First, they

Pumpkins (above), a kind of squash, and corn (left), one of the "three sisters"

planted corn kernels and piled earth over them. Then they added squash and bean seeds to this mound. When the corn grew up, the stalk held up the bean plants and the squash vines.

Many other crops, like sunflowers and amaranth, were also grown. Every region had its own way of planting, caring for, harvesting, and storing their crops.

Many kinds of tools were used in the fields. Along the East Coast, shells were turned into hoes. On the Plains, women hoed with the bone of the shoulder blade of a buffalo fastened to a stick.

This Iroquois hoe is made from an elk antler.

In the Southwest, where men worked the fields, smoothed stone blades were used.

In the dry Southwest, water was brought to the fields in ditches connected to a stream or spring. If the area was too dry for irrigation, everyone carried water to the plants in clay pots.

# Growing Corn

The first Europeans to come to North American found corn already growing here. Then, it was gathered, husked, and stored by hand. It also had to be kept away from animals.

Corn is still grown all across North America, by American Indians and others. Machines may process it, or people may gather it into decorative bunches.

However it is gathered, corn is still an important food. It makes corn flakes, feed for animals, corn on the cob, and if it's blue, it makes a batter that bakes into delicious paper-thin bread called piki.

# Harvesting and Storing

When the corn was ready for harvest, a special ritual thanked the corn. Then everyone, including children, worked long and hard to bring in the harvest.

Crops were stored in clean and dry places. In the East and South, these were deep pits dug into the ground, big enough for a person to stand inside. The walls were lined with dried grass and bark to keep out moisture. The seeds and fruits, sometimes in skin or bark bags, were carefully stacked around the sides.

When this cache pit was full, it was covered over and the opening hidden. Only the people who built the pit knew where it was located to keep it secret in case of enemy attack.

To store seeds in dry containers, women developed the art of making pottery. Every tribe and region had its own way to turn clay into pots, bowls, and jars.

The ceiling and rafters of a house were also used to store food. Squash and pumpkins were cut into rings or long strips. These were hung in mats from the ceiling. There they dried slowly in the air and smoke. Fish was also cured in

Pueblo potters are famous for their beautiful work (above). Slices of pumpkin dry (right).

the same way. Corn was piled up in rows along the walls. Beans were kept in jars.

# Living Well

Many foods were given to the world by the natives of North America, including favorites like turkey, cranberries, vanilla, and chocolate.

Many kinds of berries, cactus berries, cactus fruits, ferns, maple syrup, nuts, pawpaws, pecans, persimmons, pine

nuts, sassafras bark, strawber-
ries, wild rice, and yuccas
were gathered from nature.

A woman gathers squash from the field (above). Children display the many foods they have grown (left).

From the farmers came avocados, beans, chilies, corn, gherkins, guavas, manioc, papayas, peanuts, peppers, pineapples, plantains, potatoes, pumpkins, squashes, sunflowers, and sunroots.

American Indians were good conservationists because they took only what they needed with skill and care. They used methods proved over centuries. They learned from nature. They lived well without causing pollution or extinctions.

# To Find Out More

Here are some additional resources to help you learn more about American Indian foods:

 **Books**

 **Organizations**

Henry, Edna. **Native American Cookbook.** Julian Messner, 1983.

Liptak, Karen. **North American Indian Survival Skills.** Franklin Watts, 1990.

Penner, Lucille Recht. **A Native American Feast.** Macmillan, 1994.

Regguinti, Gordon. **The Sacred Harvest: Ojibway Wild Rice Gathering.** Lerner Publications, 1992.

**American Indian Community House, Inc.**
404 Lafayette Street
New York, NY
212-598-0100

**American Indian Heritage Foundation**
6051 Arlington Blvd.
Falls Church, VA  22044
202-463-4267

**National Museum of the American Indian**
George Gustav Heye
  Center
One Bowling Green
New York, NY
212-668-6624

## Online Sites

**Index of Native American Resources on the Internet**
*http://hanksville.phast. umass.edu/misc/ NAresources.html*

Resources on every aspect of American Indian life and culture.

**Native American Foods — Recipes**
*http://indy4.fdl.cc.mn.us/ ~isk/food/recipes.html*

Information about many American Indian foods and recipes.

**Native Food List**
*http://web.maxwell.syr.edu/ nativeweb/listserv/ natfood.html*

This page gives information on how to subscribe to a native foods e-mail discussion.

# Important Words

*cache pit* a specially made hole where foods are stored

*crop* a plant grown for food

*customs* the typical things a group of people does

*harpoon* a spear used in hunting, with a barbed point

*harvest* to gather a food from the fields where it grows

*homeland* an area where someone has lived for a long time

*irrigation* to move water around in ditches to water crops

*staple* a main food that people usually eat

# Index

# Meet the Author

Jay Miller lives in Seattle, visiting nearby reservations, mountains, streams, and the Pacific Ocean. He enjoys eating salmon and pie, hiking in the mountains, and kayaking along the shore as much as he enjoys being a writer, professor, and lecturer. He has taught in colleges in the United States and Canada. He belongs to the Delaware Wolf clan. His family is delightful and very complex. He has also authored *American Indian Families*, *American Indian Festivals*, and *American Indian Games* for the True Book series.